GYPSUM PLASTER

GYPSUM PLASTER
Its manufacture and use

Andrew Coburn, Eric Dudley and Robin Spence
Cambridge Architectural Research Ltd.

Intermediate Technology Publications 1989

IBSN 1 85339 038 0

Intermediate Technology Publications
103/105 Southampton Row
London WC1B 4HH, UK

© Intermediate Technology Publications 1989

Printed in the UK by Redwood Burn Ltd.

Contents

Glossary   43

Selected bibliography   45

Contact addresses   47

Case studies

Why use gypsum plaster?

'Successful production can, however, by no means guarantee actual acceptance in the building industry. We often receive visits from the local craftsman: they run the plaster through their fingers and knock on the demonstration blocks, they scrape their finger nails over the plastering on the walls of the plant site. Yet they remain sceptical: they want to see houses made from the new material, they want to know how it will stand up to the rainy season and what it will look like in ten years time. They are right to be cautious - it is after all, they who are held responsible if the material they use proves inadequate.'

Gypsum Production: a manual - Projecto de Gêsso 1979

Gypsum plaster is a well-proven binding material with a wide range of uses in building. It is made from raw materials which are abundant in some parts of the world and are often under-utilized. The processing technology involved in converting the raw material, *gypsum,* into the end product *gypsum plaster* is simple and suitable for small-scale operation. The energy consumption is much less than that of alternative binding materials, such as Portland cement, and a wide variety of fuels may be used. For all these reasons, there has been in recent years a growing interest in the potential for the establishment of small-scale gypsum plaster production in developing countries where raw materials are available, and where other binders are expensive and in short supply.

Much of the recent experience has been in North Africa, particularly in the Sahelian countries where extensive gypsum deposits are found. Out of this experience, numerous papers and reports have been published and the Paris-based intermediate technology group GRET *(Groupe de Recherche et d'Echanges Technologiques)* has published a technical manual on gypsum plaster production and use. However, many of these documents are in French, and to date no brief introduction to the subject has been available in English.

This publication is intended as a first attempt to fill this gap in the available literature on low-cost building materials. It is in no sense intended as a comprehensive guide to the full range of techniques of manufacture and use of gypsum plaster. Rather it is intended to serve three purposes:

* To offer potential *producers* of gypsum plaster an outline of the range of manufacturing techniques available, their requirements and characteristics.
* To offer potential *users* of gypsum plaster a guide to the range of its possible uses, the properties required, and the limitations.
* To provide an introduction for industrial development planners in government or in aid agencies to the potential for increased exploitation of currently under-utilized deposits of gypsum.

The information given is summarized from a range of sources in addition to the author's own experience. These sources are listed at the end, and addresses are also given of the principal organizations involved in the promotion of small-scale gypsum exploitation to help those interested to obtain further more detailed assistance.

Gypsum or gypsum plaster?

The term *gypsum* is properly used for the naturally occurring mineral, a rock from which the building material discussed in this publication is derived. To distinguish it from the raw material, the processed building material is always referred to here as *gypsum plaster*. It may be thought that this use of the term could lead to some confusion, since plastering in building is only one of the potential uses for gypsum plaster. Other uses for gypsum plaster are for concrete, block-making, and fibre-board production. However, the authors consider that the use of the term *gypsum* for both the raw material and the processed building material, which is sometimes done in the English literature, is even more confusing.

In this respect the English language is less precise than the French, in which *'gypse'* for the raw material and simply *'plâtre'* for the gypsum plaster are clearly distinguished. The English term plaster generally refers to wall renders made from a variety of materials including lime and Portland cement.

These terms, along with others which commonly cause confusion, are defined in the glossary at the end of this publication.

Gypsum plaster — a well proven technology

It is probable that gypsum plaster was the earliest deliberately manufactured cementitious binder. Walls in the pyramids of Giza, which date from 2,200 BC, and in temples from Persia to Crete made extensive use of gypsum plaster. A pupil of the ancient Greek philosopher Plato recorded its uses in Cyprus, Phoenicia and Syria. The gypsum plaster used in many ancient sites is still in good condition today as are the *frescoes* which are painted on to gypsum plaster surfaces.

In northern Europe, gypsum plaster is best known from its association with France. The extraction began near Paris in Roman times and in the 13th century was described in detail in Etienne Boileau's *Book of Trades*. In England gypsum plaster was referred to as plaster of Paris. As early as the 9th century it was used in Rochester cathedral mixed with bull's blood to improve its workability. By the sixteenth century the British were improving their plaster with egg whites and residues from beer production, while the French of Rouen explored the possibilities of urine.

A great expansion of gypsum exploitation in Paris came in 1667 when an ordinance was passed in the wake of a series of serious fires. It became obligatory to cover the timber frames of houses with nailed laths and gypsum plaster inside and outside. This led to both an expansion of production and a refinement of skills in the application of plaster. By the 18th century entire façades were rendered in imitation of stone with elaborate stucco work.

The use of gypsum plaster

The greatest use of gypsum plaster in the building industry today is in renders and finishes for internal use, including plasterboard. But gypsum plaster is a very versatile material and it is increasingly used in a wider range of applications. As a binding material, it can be considered in strategies for substitution of Portland cement in applications which do not need the very high strength that Portland cement can develop.

The technology of gypsum plaster production is simple and, due to its long history, techniques are relatively well proven. In many countries deposits of rock gypsum are considerably underexploited, either because deposits are localized or, more commonly, because traditional uses of gypsum plaster in buildings have fallen out of favour with the advent of modern materials, in particular Portland cement.

Yet gypsum plaster has a number of advantages over alternative materials based on Portland cement and lime:

- it does not shrink when it dries, so plastered walls do not crack and fine details may be achieved in mouldings;
- it dries and hardens quickly, so a second finishing coat of plaster may be applied promptly;
- in its manufacture the raw material must be heated for a short time to a temperature of only around 160°C, whereas lime requires 900° to 1,100°C and Portland cement is formed at 1,450°C. This means that gypsum plaster requires simpler technology and considerably less fuel; and
- it is naturally fire resistant.

However, unlike Portland cement, gypsum plaster is a *non-hydraulic setting binder*. That is to say that even after the gypsum plaster has set it is still slightly soluble in water, hence it should not be used externally except in the most arid locations. Nor should it be used internally in excessively humid rooms without suitable protection. There are also limitations to its use structurally since the strengths achieved by gypsum plaster are not as high as with Portland cement or lime. But strengths are entirely adequate for one or two storey construction.

Gypsum plaster is, then, a possibility particularly worth considering where there are readily available sources of raw gypsum and Portland cement is expensive and/or in short supply. If there is, in addition, an arid climate, the use of gypsum plaster is likely to be economically favourable, since it may be possible to use it for unrendered blocks or as an external rendering material.

Manufacture

---

1. Raw gypsum

Gypsum plaster consists of a mixture of three related chemicals, calcium sulphate *dihydrate*($CaSO_4.2H_2O$), calcium sulphate *hemi-hydrate* ($CaSO_4.\frac{1}{2}H_2O$), and calcium sulphate *anhydrite* ($CaSO_4$). The different proportions of these three chemicals determine the plaster's properties. In some plasters one or two of the three chemicals are reduced to nothing, for instance plaster of Paris is pure hemi-hydrate, while Keene's plaster is pure anhydrite. All three of these occur in nature, although the hemi-hydrate is rare. At depth, under pressure and heat, the dihydrate becomes anhydrite while near the surface the dihydrate is by far the most common. The natural mineral whose principal constituent is dihydrate is known as *gypsum*. It is important to remember that gypsum is the name for the natural raw material while gypsum plaster refers to the manufactured powder which can be used for a variety of purposes apart from plastering itself (see the section on uses in building).

A) Types of raw gypsum
Gypsum can be formed through a number of geological processes, hence it occurs in nature in various forms. These forms can be roughly divided into two principal types: rock gypsum and gypsum sand.

i. Rock gypsum
Rock Gypsum is the most commonly occurring form of gypsum. It is a rock usually formed through the evaporation of salt water. It can occur in strata from only a few centimetres in thickness to tens of metres. Typically it will be found over, or alternating with, shale and limestone, including chalk and soapstone, and under rock salt. It can also occur with sulphur and clay.

It is a crystalline mineral yet with a soapy texture. It is usually white, though it can be slightly grey, yellow, pink or brown. Geologists distinguish various varieties of rock gypsum. The most famous is alabaster, traditionally used for carving and occasionally to make windows.

By appearance, to the inexperienced eye, rock gypsum can be confused with other crystals found in similar circumstances, commonly calcite (the main ingredient of limestone), dolomite, quartz and anhydrite. However, unlike these its surface may be readily scratched with a fingernail. Also, a crystal of gypsum if held over a flame will turn cloudy and opaque and give off water.

ii. Gypsum sand

The other common source of gypsum is gypsum sand, also known as aeolian gypsum, which consists of beds or sand dunes of wind-blown powder. In arid areas these can form a harsh solid crust. These areas are usually useless for agriculture, but some plants do grow on such crusts and can be useful for confirming that a soil is rich in gypsum. These plants are referred to by botanists as *gypsophytes* (plants that need gypsum) and *gypsoclines* (plants which tolerate gypsum).

One of the problems of gypsum sand is that it is rarely as pure as rock gypsum, often being mixed with other wind-blown minerals. In some cases it may require cleaning to decontaminate it for use as a building material. For instance, a variety of gypsum sand known as gypsite is a very fine form of gypsum mixed with clay and marl which is usually found overlying deposits of coarser gypsum sand. Gypsite may contain as little as 60 per cent gypsum. Because of this degree of impurity gypsite is usually not used as a building material but may be used for agriculture, as an additive to soils which are deficient in calcium or sulphur, or which are alkaline or have been reclaimed from the sea. However, there are many places where cleaner, untapped deposits of gypsum sand exist near or on the surface. In a project in the Cape Verde Islands (see case study 3) the surface deposits were found to be 95-98 per cent pure. In such circumstances small-scale gypsum plaster producers can set up business with a minimal investment of time and money *(see section 3Bii on flat-plate kilns)*. For such producers gypsum sand is a more attractive proposition than rock gypsum.

B) Sources

Gypsum is found and mined in all the continents. Its principal uses are in the production of plasterboard and as an additive in Portland cement production. At present the United States of America is the largest producer of gypsum, producing nearly twice as much as her nearest rival, France. Estimates of current *known* reserves places 86 per cent of gypsum resources in Europe and North America. Yet there is reason to believe that many unacknowledged reserves exist in the developing world. High-grade gypsum sands are found in many arid countries of North Africa and the Middle East. Much of this is in deposits that can be easily worked and processed with technologies that require very low capital investment. In these countries, characterized by low rainfall, the potential application of gypsum plaster in the building industry is much wider than many other places, as the susceptibility of gypsum plaster to humidity is much less of a problem than elsewhere.

Gypsum is produced as a by-product, in the form of phospho-gypsum, in the manufacture of phosphoric acid, which is used for fertilizers. Also it may be a by-product of salt production, and of the cleaning process of desulphurizing exhaust fumes from power stations. Waste product gypsum is often offered for sale to the building industry at extremely favourable prices. However, by-product gypsum usually contains impurities which may need expensive decontamination or neutralizing before it can be used to produce building plaster.

The presence of a Portland cement industry may indicate the presence of gypsum, though, since Portland cement consists of only 5 per cent gypsum, it may be imported.

2. Gypsum plaster

A) The chemistry of plaster

Heating the prepared raw gypsum forces a chemical reaction in the gypsum to change it from dihydrate, $CaSO_4.2H_2O$, to hemi-hydrate, $CaSO_4.\frac{1}{2}H_2O$, by driving off $1\frac{1}{2}$ of the molecules of water, known as the *water of crystallization*. This process of chemical change through heating is known as *calcining* and the resulting hemi-hydrate is the chief constituent of most gypsum plasters.

i. Hemi-hydrate α and β

There are two types of hemi-hydrate known as α and β. The α form is produced under pressure in a humid atmosphere which results in an even crystalline structure. When the hemi-hydrate is produced at atmospheric pressure the crystal water is driven off as steam, which disrupts the crystalline structure resulting in the fragmentary crystals of β hemi-hydrate. The principal differences in their practical characteristics are that β requires more water to make a plaster and the resulting plaster will set more quickly and be weaker. There are also a series of plasters between α and β with intermediate properties. Hemi-hydrate β is the most commonly used form and is the only type produced by small-scale low-cost production technologies.

ii. Setting

The chemical change of calcination is reversible by simply adding water. This process is known as *hydration*. The molecules of water combine with those of the hemi-hydrate to create crystals of dihydrate. As the process of hydration begins the crystals are in *suspension,* that is they are floating freely in the liquid of the plaster slurry. As the long thin crystals grow there comes a point at which the crystals start to interfere with each other, joining up to form a crystal matrix. The individual crystals can no longer move freely in the solution. This is known as the *initial set.* The process of hydration is still going on in the interstices of the matrix until such time as all the hemi-hydrate is used up. That moment is the *final set.* For all practical purposes the amount of water added to the dry plaster must be more than the water actually necessary for hydration. Hence, the plaster will set, that is hydration will be complete, before it has actually dried out.

iii. Acceleration and retardation

The initial set clearly does not occur simultaneously in all parts of the plaster; there is a more or less gradual process of stiffening. The setting process can be seen as four moments dividing the process into three distinct periods:

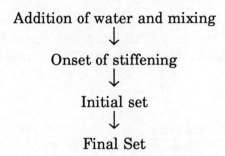

Addition of water and mixing
↓
Onset of stiffening
↓
Initial set
↓
Final Set

Through the intentional use of additives and the accidental effects of impurities the lengths of these three periods may be altered to produce plasters to suit different needs and working practices. These chemicals, for obvious reasons, are called accelerators and retarders. The most important accelerator is gypsum itself. Particles of gypsum (dihydrate) in the plaster slurry act as seeds around which the crystals will rapidly grow. For this reason it is very important to keep tools and containers scrupulously clean of old dried plaster. The hydration process for anhydrite goes through two stages, first to hemi-hydrate, then to dihydrate. Hence, anhydrite which often occurs naturally with gypsum or which is produced by 'over-burning' in the calcination process is an important retarder.

In addition to the use of gypsum and anhydrite to manipulate the hydration process there are a range of chemicals which more subtly effect the setting times. No hard and fast rules can be laid down since the effects of additives are themselves effected by the natural impurities present in the plaster. To determine the most appropriate additives the user must decide on the desired setting characteristics and then test the locally available product (see case study 1).

B) Types of plaster

The gypsum plasters that a peasant farmer uses to finish his house, that a craftsman uses to make a decorative moulding, or that an industrialist uses to make plasterboard are not all the same. As we have seen, each one is a distinct mixture of chemicals, some there for a purpose, some as impurities. Before considering how to make gypsum plaster the user must decide *which* type of plaster is required. The general characteristics of some types of plaster are set out below.

i. Ash plaster

Principal uses: *rendering of walls and ceilings*
                    mortar
                    agriculture

Ash plaster is a rustic plaster that contains a mixture of hemi-hydrate, anhydrite and raw gypsum as well as many impurities, in particular ash from burnt solid fuel. Typically the mixture will contain around 50 per cent hemi-hydrate. The small amount of anhydrite is useful since it slows down the otherwise rapid setting process. The initial set will usually happen within two or three minutes, while full hardness may take some days to achieve. However, if there are not too many impurities, the final plaster can be very hard and may have a crushing strength of the order of 30 kg/cm^2.

In many parts of the world ash plaster, also known as *timchent* or *goss*, has, for many centuries, been the only plaster available and can be perfectly suitable for mortar and plaster work where a particularly high quality of finish is not required.

ii. Plaster of Paris

    Principal uses: *intricate castings*
                                     dental and medical casts
                                     repairs
                                     plasterboard manufacture

Plaster of Paris is the common name for pure, or nearly pure, hemi-hydrate. It sets extremely quickly and so its uses in day-to-day building are limited. However, its fast setting can be useful in industrialized manufacturing of prefabricated elements such as plasterboard, though in modern plasterboard manufacture chemical accelerators are used to speed up the drying even further. Its main potential use in developing countries would be for the manufacture of precast and reinforced units (see case study 6).

iii. Retarded hemi-hydrate gypsum plaster

    Principal uses: *modern commercial building plaster*

This is the main commercial building plaster. It is plaster of Paris, that is hemi-hydrate, whose setting time has been lengthened with the use of chemical additives. This makes it easier to use than plaster of Paris. There are a whole range of commercial additives, a common one being keratin, made from hoof and horn meal. A plaster containing 0.8 per cent keratin and 5 per cent lime will remain workable for about two hours and then suddenly harden up in twenty minutes or so. Citric acid is a retarder which does not require the presence of lime, whereas lactose, maltose, and sucrose are all retarders like keratin which require some lime in the mix. Other commonly used retarders include: borax, sugar, molasses, and sodium citrate (see case study 1).

However, as with ash plaster, the most important additive is anhydrite. A good general purpose plaster for rendering walls and ceilings can be obtained from a mixture of 50 to 70 per cent hemi-hydrate with 30 to 50 per cent anhydrite.

As with plaster of Paris, retarded hemi-hydrate plasters can not be kept workable by adding more water. Once they start to harden the process is final.

iv. Anhydrous gypsum plaster

    Principal uses: *Wall and ceiling plastering particularly where either a very flat finish is required or a patterned surface.*

Anhydrous plasters, as the name suggests, are primarily made from anhydrite, though they contain a certain amount of hemi-hydrate. The presence of hemi-hydrate means they have a rapid early set, but full setting takes considerably longer, allowing for more work to be done by the plasterer which can be useful where a very smooth finish, or a specially patterned surface is required. Anhydrous plasters may also be *knocked back*, that is to say within the first hour or so more water may be added to maintain the workability.

v. Keene's plaster

   Principal uses: *plastering where a very hard finish is required*

Keene's plaster is the name for anhydrous plaster with no hemi-hydrate. It has a slow continuous set which allows a skilled craftsman to achieve a very smooth finish capable of taking gloss paint. The finished surface is very hard and was traditionally used for dados and exposed corners.

3. Tests and standards

Standards are always a relative concept. The specifics of what constitutes 'good standards' depends on the context, specifically the type of producer and the type of market. Formalized standards do not exist for ash plaster, but that is not to say that 'good quality' ash plaster does not exist. The famous plaster industry in Paris in the 18th and 19th centuries was founded upon the production of ash plaster.

There is no substitute for the craftsman's experience of what is, and what is not, a good or adequate material. The purpose of outlining here some simple tests is to allow the field worker or entrepreneur to gauge the quality of the gypsum plaster they are producing and to recognize natural gypsum.

A) Recognizing gypsum

i. Specific gravity

Rock gypsum can be confused with a number of other similar looking crystalline rocks. Gypsum has a relatively low density. A simple test can be carried out to determine the density, or *specific gravity*, of a sample of rock, that is, how many grams does one cubic centimetre (one millilitre) weigh. To do this you need: scales with metric weights, a small measuring jug measured off in millilitres (ml or cc), and a large, wide topped glass or plastic container, like a storage jar or a larger measuring jug.

Once you have obtained a good solid crystalline sample small enough to fit into the bottom half of the larger container but otherwise as big as possible, carry out the following procedure:

1 The sample must be completely dry, if the sample is damp it would be best to dry it out completely by leaving it out in the sun for a few days, or put it in a *very low temperature* oven),
2 Weigh the rock sample, record the weight in **grams**.
3 Pour cold water into the empty container until it is approximately half full.
4 Carefully mark the level of the water on the outside of the container, this is usually easier if you stick a strip of masking tape up the side of the container so that you have something to write on.
5 Place the rock sample into the water so that it is completely submerged and mark the new level of the water.
7 Remove the sample from the water and if necessary top the water up to bring it up to its original level.
8 Using the fine measuring jug, add water until the level reaches the second and higher mark. Record how much water had to be added in **millilitres**. The volume of added water is the same as the volume of the sample.
9 Divide the weight of the sample by its volume (the volume of the water in millilitres), the result is the *specific gravity* of the sample. If the sample is rock gypsum the specific gravity should come out to be approximately 2.3. The specific gravity of other crystalline rocks which can get confused with gypsum are: calcite 2.72, dolomite 2.85, anhydrite 2.95 and quartz 2.65.

ii. Dissolving

Gypsum sand, and also powdered rock gypsum, may be identified by dissolving it in hot water or if available in hydrochloric acid. For instance, if a litre of clean fresh water (preferably distilled) is heated to between 25°C and 40°C then two grams of gypsum should be able to dissolve completely (two grams of fine gypsum sand will be about equivalent to a 5 ml spoonful). In salt water a greater quantity will dissolve.

B) Testing gypsum plaster

Using relatively low-cost equipment, which many material laboratories in developing countries will already possess, standard numerical tests can be carried out to describe the physical characteristics of gypsum plasters. The relevance of each test will depend on the particular applications for which the plaster will be used. Typical of these tests are those described in the Indian Standard 2542 (part I) - 1964. The equipment used in these tests is standardized and may be obtained from many suppliers of laboratory equipment. Some addresses of such suppliers are given at the back of this publication. In summary these tests are:

i. Consistency

Consistency is measure of the water to dry plaster ratio in a freshly mixed batch of plaster. If there is insufficient water the plaster slurry will be too stiff for practical use and in the extreme not all the plaster will undergo the chemical transformation of setting. But if there is too much water the surplus water will occupy space before eventually evaporating and leaving a low density and, hence, weak plaster. For any plaster there is, therefore, an optimum or 'normal' consistency.

To determine the consistency a plunger rod, both clean and wet, of a specific weight (50 g) and cross-section (19 mm diameter) is held so as to be just touching the surface of a sample of freshly mixed liquid plaster. The plunger is released and the penetration distance into the mix is recorded. This distance is taken as a measure of mixture consistency. When the plunger penetrates by 30 ± 2 mm the plaster is considered to have a 'normal' consistency. This normal consistency is then expressed as the number of millilitres of water which should be added to 100 mg of dry plaster to achieve that consistency. In all the tests, (except the next one) the plaster used should be of this 'normal' consistency.

> *Equipment needed:* The 'Vicat' apparatus, modified so as to have a flat based plunger, 19 mm diameter, rather than the normal needle. A conical ring mould of non-corroding, non-absorbant material with a base diameter of 7 cm and a top diameter of 6 cm and a height of 4 cm. A 10 cm square glass base plate with a thin coating of petroleum jelly.

ii. Freedom from coarse particles.

To achieve a smooth and homogeneous finish to a plastered surface it is important that the plaster is relatively free of coarse particles. To determine the coarse particle content a 100 g sample of dry plaster is sieved for five minutes, using a 1.18 mm sieve. Lumps may be broken up with fingers but they should not be rubbed on the sieve. The weight of the residue in grams is the percentage of coarse particles. The percentages considered appropriate under British Standard 1191 are:

Plaster of Paris	5 %
Retarded hemi-hydrate	3 %
Anhydrous plaster	1 %
Keene's plaster	1 %

iii. Bending or transverse strength

A plaster's strength in bending is of particular importance in the use of plaster-board or other prefabricated panels since they are usually used to span and so they utilize the plaster structurally to resist transverse loads.

Six small beams of plaster are prepared, each one being 25 mm x 25 mm x 100 mm. The preparation of the beams is different for each type of plaster:

Plaster type	Mix by weight	Curing
Plaster of Paris	3 plaster, 2 lime	Left to dry for two hours before being de-moulded then tested immediately.
Retarded hemi-hydrate	1 plaster, 3 clean sand	24 hours in the moulds under damp conditions; de-moulded; dried for three days in an oven at 35° - 40°C then immediately tested.
Anhydrous	3 plaster, 1 lime, 9 clean sand	24 hours in moulds under damp conditions; demoulded; three days under damp conditions; three days in oven at 35° - 40°C then immediately tested.
Keene's plaster	1 plaster, 3 clean sand	As anhydrous plaster

The beam is supported at 75 mm centres on rollers 12.5 mm in diameter with a central point load, in the form of another roller. The load is applied at a rate of 22.5 to 90 kg per minute until failure. The result is expressed in terms of the modulus of rupture in N/mm^2, which in this case may be calculated by multiplying the failure load in kilograms by 0.00706. The experiment should be repeated six times and an average modulus obtained.

Equipment needed: *Moulds of 25 ± 0.4 mm square cross section, 100 mm long of well-greased non-corrodible metal. A loading machine. Two 12.5 mm dia. roller supports and a third roller for the load. A humid cupboard giving at least 80 per cent relative humidity at a temperature of 27° ± 2°C.*

iv. Mechanical resistance

The mechanical resistance is a measure of a plastered wall's resistance to impacts. This is particularly important in public buildings and circulation spaces where walls are frequently knocked.

Four beams are prepared, as in the previous test. A ball bearing is dropped from a height of 1.82 m onto one of the surfaces of the beam which was formed by the mould. The ball bearing, in practice, is dropped down a vertical tube 16 mm in diameter and 1.72 m long which comes to an end 100 mm above the surface of the beam. The diameter of the impression made is measured and then measured again at right angles to the first measurement. The test is repeated on the opposite face of the same beam and then on the remaining three beams, giving in all 16 measurements (eight impressions each with two diameters). These results are then averaged, disregarding any obvious anomalies. British standard 1191 gives the following diameters:

Plaster of Paris	none specified
Retarded hemi-hydrate	5 mm
Anhydrous	4.5 mm
Keene's plaster	4 mm

Equipment needed: *A clean and polished steel ball 12.7 mm in diameter, weighing 8.33 g. Beam moulds and a humid cupboard as in the test above for transverse strength.*

v. Setting time

As mentioned earlier, plaster of Paris has a very short setting time which can limit its usefulness to the builder, though on occasions it can be a useful property. The optimum setting time is purely a product of the user's needs and convenience. The setting time of a plaster can be controlled through the use of additives and determined with the following technique (see also Case Study 1 opposite).

200 g of plaster is mixed with water sufficient to give a 'normal' consistency (see consistency test above). The time at which the plaster is added to the water is recorded. The plaster is placed into the conical ring mould and put under the Vicat apparatus, which itself is in the humid cupboard. Every few minutes the needle of the Vicat apparatus is placed touching the surface of the plaster and released. The sample is then moved slightly to avoid subsequent tests hitting the same point. When the needle can be released and it does not reach the bottom of the mould, setting time is considered to have been reached.

Equipment needed: *A 'Vicat' apparatus (a vertical plunger of weight 300 ± 0.5 g with, at the bottom, a needle 1 ± 0.05 mm in diameter and 50 mm long). A conical mould, 70 ± 3 mm diameter at the base, 60 ± 3 mm at the top, and 40 ± 1 mm deep. A greased glass base plate. A humid cupboard.*

CASE STUDY 1: — Field testing retarders

Generally the use of retarders has been seen as only applicable to advanced gypsum plaster industries with the benefit of sophisticated laboratories. Yet, many of the common retarders, such as keratin, lactose, sucrose, and citric acid, are chemicals readily available from natural sources.

R.G.Smith of the Building Research Establishment in the U.K. has described a simple method of obtaining keratin and of testing its qualities as a retarder. In Britain keratin is obtained from hoofs and horns, but it can also be extracted from fish bones. On the Cape Verde Islands experiments were carried out in which tuna fish bones were chopped up and boiled for half an hour and then cooled.

A mix of two parts plaster and one part water was put in two polythene bags, one with the fish liquor the other without. The bags were sealed and shaken for one minute. The polythene bags made ideal containers, first because they were quite clean, so the plaster would not get contaminated, but also because one could readily judge the process of hardening, simply by touch. Four distinct states are identifiable, 'liquid', 'stiffening', 'crackable', and 'rigid'.

The experiment was repeated using tree resin ground to a powder, which was also found to have a retarding effect. Using this simple technique with various materials in various proportions untrained field workers or entrepreneurs with no special equipment can design their own retarded plasters using the materials most suitable for their context.

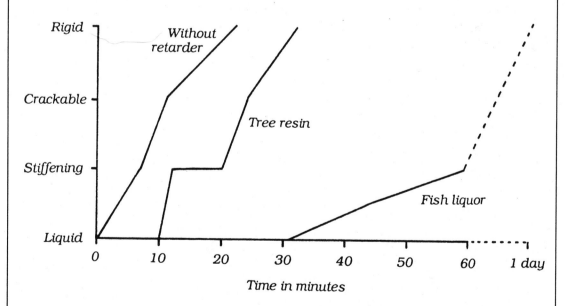

Results of elementary field tests carried out by R.G.Smith in the Cape Verde Islands

vi. Expansion on setting

Many cementitious materials, such as Portland cement, shrink with setting, but gypsum plaster slightly expands. Some additives to plaster can increase the amount of expansion and lead to a reduction in strength.

To determine the expansion the trough of an extensometer should be lined with thin paper, and then filled with fresh plaster of a normal consistency. The whole apparatus is put into the humid cupboard and left until no further expansion is taking place. The expansion recorded in millimetres gives the percentage linear expansion. This is only specified for retarded hemi-hydrate plaster, the acceptable level being 0.2 per cent.

> *Equipment needed:*   *An extensometer with a V-shaped cradle 100 mm long, 55 mm wide, and 25 mm deep with a rounded point to the V, one end is fixed while the other operates a micrometer gauge sensitive to 0.01 mm. A humid cupboard as described above.*

vii. Soundness

If a plaster has impurities or is not homogeneous, then with time and humidity the plaster can deteriorate through a process of continuing chemical change. To check a plaster's 'soundness' samples are exposed to heat and humidity.

Pats of plaster are prepared in ring moulds. If they are of plaster of Paris or retarded hemi-hydrate they should stand in the humid cupboard for 16 to 24 hours, whereas anhydrous and Keene's plaster should stand in the cupboard for three days. The samples, without being removed from the moulds, are subjected to steam at atmospheric pressure for three hours. Care should be taken that condensed water does not fall back onto the plaster. The physical appearance of the samples is examined. It is required that there should be no signs of disintegration, popping or pitting on the their surfaces.

> *Equipment needed:*   *Well-greased ring moulds 100 mm in diameter and 6 mm deep. A greased glass base plate. A humid cupboard as described above. A steamer.*

viii. Compressive strength of set plaster.

In the manufacture of plasterboard and of plaster for conventional wet plastering the compressive strength is not particularly important. However, in recent developments in which gypsum plaster is used as a binder in the manufacture of blocks it can be important to know the compressive strength of the material.

A quantity of dry gypsum plaster with twice its weight of clean sand is mixed with water to a 'normal' consistency (see above test) and used to cast six standard cubes. These are immediately placed in a moist atmosphere (90 to 100 per cent humidity) where they should remain for at least 24 hours. The cubes are then dried in an oven at 30° to 40°C until they have reached a constant weight, but for no longer than a week. Finally they are placed in a desiccator for 24 hours over magnesium perchlorate. Immediately afterwards they are tested to destruction in a loading machine, the load being applied across two of the faces which were formed by the faces of the mould. The result is the average of the tests, though if one or two of the cubes vary from the average by more than 15 per cent they are discarded. The required compressive strength depends on the use to which the gypsum plaster mixture is to be put.

Equipment needed: *Six split cube moulds of non-corrodible material of sides 50 ± 0.5 mm with a maximum surface variation of 0.05 mm. The angular deviation between sides is 90 ± 0.05°. A glass or metal base plate coated with petroleum jelly. An oven with air circulation. A desiccator. A loading machine which can apply loads at a rate between 1 to 4 kg/cm² per second.*

ix. Chemical tests

In addition to the physical tests, the British Standard BS1191 sets out tests to determine the chemical characteristics of the plasters. These require relatively sophisticated techniques which we shall not detail here, but the aims of these tests are to determine such things as:

• Chemical purity

Chemical analysis of the composition of the plaster determines the proportion of 'impurities'. Many of these extra substances can enhance the properties of the plaster for given situations, for instance, in Britain some commercial finishing plasters contain as much as 20 per cent clay.

• Chemical ratios

The ratios between chemicals can alter the qualities of the plaster, for instance, calcium oxide should not normally be less than two thirds of the sulphur trioxide level.

• Control of levels of soluble salts.

To stop efflorescence in finished renders the level of soluble salts must be kept down. The most harmful salts are those of magnesium, potassium, and sodium. Standards require that, in a chemical analysis, the proportions by weight of MgO, K_2O, and Na_2O should not exceed 2 %, 0.1 %, and 0.02 % respectively.

It should be emphasized that all the 'acceptable' results given in the above tests are still based on the standards of the highly industrialized countries, in particular, the United States (ASTM C472 — American Society for Testing and Materials), United Kingdom (BS1191 — British Standards Institute), and Canada (CSA A82.20 — Canadian Standards Association). Work still remains to be done using test methods such as the ones above to identify results that can be considered as acceptable intermediate standards.

4. Production technologies

The technologies used to produce gypsum plaster depend on a number of factors:
- The type and quality of the desired finished product
- The type and quality of the raw gypsum
- The size of the market
- The type of producer

The technologies described over the following pages are not all suitable, or necessary, for all situations. Any selection made from these technologies must be made on the basis of a consideration of the actual circumstances.

A) Extraction

Since gypsum sand occurs on or near the surface it can be easily dug out using conventional spades or mechanical diggers. Gypsum rock is relatively soft, especially when underground and with a high moisture content. For centuries rock gypsum has been cut by hand, using pick axes. In mechanized extraction, the rock is excavated by explosive blasting and scooping with a mechanical digger. Manual extraction gives much more regularly shaped and more homogeneous sizes of blocks than mechanical, which may require further breaking up before the rock is crushed.

Most rock gypsum deposits are relatively narrow seams and occur close to or on the surface, a characteristic which permits exploitation with conventional shallow quarrying techniques, the main types of which are:

i. Open-cast mines
Surface-occurring gypsum is cut down in terraces, leaving a stepped profile to the quarry to allow progressive exploitation at a number of levels.

ii. Drift mines
Sloping access tunnels allow vehicles to be driven or drawn from the surface down to the underground workings. Subterranean galleries are exploited in pillar-and-stall configurations (leaving columns of rock gypsum standing to support the roof).

iii. Shallow shafts
Subterranean galleries can also be dug from pits or shallow shafts sunk down to the level of the deposit. The rock gypsum is winched to the surface.

B) Preparing gypsum
Gypsum has to be broken down to get even sizes of gypsum particles. The process may involve several stages including drying, crushing, screening and grinding. The manufacturer should also provide some kind of storage compound, preferably covered, to keep the plaster dry and free from impurities.

i. Drying

Before rock gypsum can be crushed to a workable size or sand gypsum passed through a sieve, it must be dry. This may involve no more than spreading the gypsum out and letting it dry under the sun. But, in practical terms this requirement obliges the manufacturer to make available sufficient land to spread out several days' worth of raw material. This drying floor should be enclosed by a low wall to stop the sand blowing away or impurities blowing in. In climates subject to a rainy season provision should be made for a roof, which will both slow down drying and significantly increase the cost of production. The alternative, in such circumstances, is for gypsum production to be a seasonal industry alternating with agriculture.

ii. Crushing

If the manufacturers are blessed with a ready supply of good quality gypsum sand there will be no need for crushing. Where the sand is in lumps and the production process is on a small scale the lumps can simply be broken down in a conventional mortar and pestle. But this is slow and onerous work. Where resources allow, the gypsum, whether as sand or rock, should be broken down with a mechanical crusher. In recent years very effective low-cost crushers have been developed (see Case Study 2 overleaf). It should be noted that in many traditional forms of plaster production, such as that practiced in Paris up until the early twentieth century, the raw rock gypsum was not crushed but placed in the kilns as rocks straight from the quarry. However, crushing the rock gypsum will result in a more uniform product when the gypsum is burnt (see section below on calcining).

iii. Screening

Where practical, gypsum should be screened, partly to remove impurities but also to try and achieve the greatest homogeneity of particle size. In very basic production such as that employed on the Cape Verde Islands (see Case Study 3), the gypsum can simply be sieved into a container like an oil drum. However, where resources allow, the system should be rationalized with a large sieve suspended from above.

iv. Grinding

To achieve the best quality the raw material should be as finely ground as possible. To achieve a fine powder a ball mill or other such mechanical mill should be used. However, this degree of sophistication would probably not be appropriate for the small manufacturer and is not necessary for the production of general purpose plaster where a high quality finish is not required. To the best of the authors' knowledge there is no evidence that gypsum dust is a health hazard.

CASE STUDY 2: U.K. — Manual crusher

J.P.M. Parry and Associates Limited developed this manually powered crusher for use on clay and shale in the production of bricks, though it is equally suitable for many other materials. The machine is operated manually by an easy pumping motion accumulating energy into a heavy swinging pendulum which then transmits the power to a pair of adjustable jaws. The material to be crushed is fed between the jaws from a hopper. It is important that the material is dry, to prevent the jaws from becoming clogged. The pendulum weight is in the form of a steel box which is filled with stone or sand on site to give it the necessary mass.

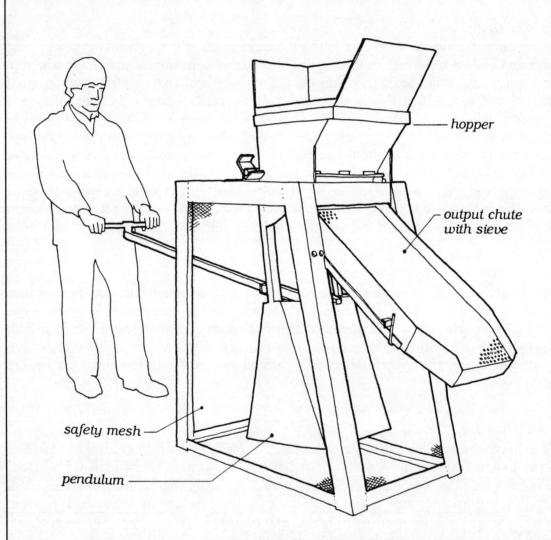

The machine comes in two sizes, the larger for 3 to 4 man operation which can produce up to 5 tonnes of material per day. The smaller machine is for one man operation and produces over one tonne per day. The quantity of output is determined, among other things, by the gap between the jaws. The above figures are for a 5 mm gap. The output chute can be fitted with a sieve to carry out the sieving automatically.

C) Calcining (heating)

Gypsum is calcined either by direct heat, by mixing it with fuel and burning the two together, or by cooking it, that is by indirectly heating it within a container.

i. Direct heating — burning

Direct heating is the technique used to make ash plaster in which the gypsum and the fuel are mixed together or share the same chamber. In such 'firing' some of the gypsum is invariably 'over-burned' (anhydrite) and some may be raw gypsum that has failed to reach calcining temperature. The amount of the gypsum that has been successfully calcined is determined by how uniform the temperatures achieved in the kiln were and the homogeneity of the pieces of gypsum being fired. (Large pieces of rock gypsum are likely to be over-burned on the outside, raw in the middle and only successfully calcined in between.). It is therefore important that the resulting burned mixture is carefully mixed together and ground to a uniform powder. Methods of directly heated calcining include:

• *Non-permanent kilns*

The crudest and oldest method of calcining gypsum is to make a bonfire from gypsum mixed with fuel and to burn the gypsum for several days. This was done either in a conical pyre, or by digging a pit into the ground (for example the traditional dug-out kilns of the Touggourt region of Algeria), or by digging a hole for fuel into surface gypsum deposits. Where an artisanal producer does not have the resources or a site for a permanent kiln, or where a field worker wants to produce some trial plaster, these techniques may be the most appropriate.

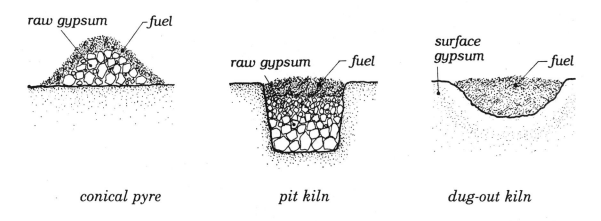

conical pyre   pit kiln   dug-out kiln

• *Permanent kilns*

A rather more effective and controllable method of burning gypsum is in a permanent kiln. In such kilns, the degree to which the raw gypsum is burned is determined by the amount of fuel mixed in with the gypsum, the length of time the kiln is fired, and the distribution of the fuel and the gypsum. The placing and grading of the different sized pieces of gypsum to allow the flow of the hot gases are relatively skilled operations. In its most elementary form, as still used in Algeria today, the kiln is formed against a rock face by an enclosing masonry wall.

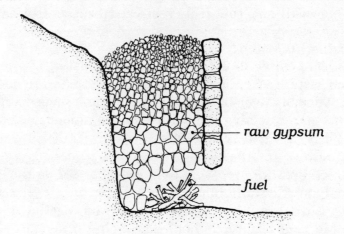

Elementary kiln

More substantial shaft kilns are also easily constructed and have been commonly used wherever gypsum occurs. A cylindrical shaft is constructed from stone or brickwork, with a small opening (an eye) at the base.

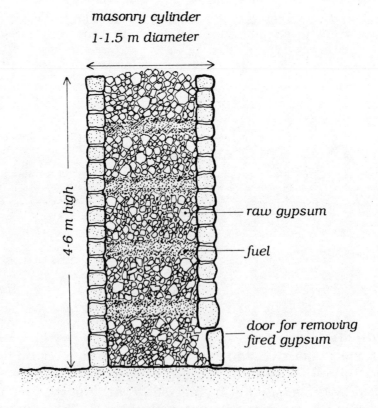

Shaft kiln

The shaft kiln is loaded from the top with alternating layers of solid fuel (usually charcoal or coal) and raw rock gypsum. After several days' firing, and after cooling, the gypsum plaster is unloaded through the eye at the base and the kiln is loaded for another batch.

Much larger batches can be fired in a walled kiln. This is a rectangular building with perforated walls for ventilation, in which gypsum is stacked for firing. Walled kilns were commonly used in many parts of Western Europe up until the 1950s and are suitable for large-volume, basic-grade gypsum plaster production. Within the large internal space of the walled kiln several crude vaults are built from the pieces of rock gypsum from the quarries. This is a relatively skilled job, and is labour-intensive. On top of the vaults, layers of gypsum are placed with smaller pieces towards the top, and finally topped by a layer of gypsum dust. The fuel is placed in the vaults and the whole construction is fired. Walled kilns can be built as large as required and can produce batches of hundreds of cubic metres of gypsum plaster at a time.

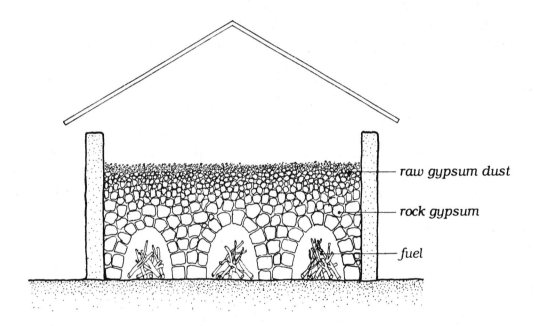

raw gypsum dust

rock gypsum

fuel

Walled kiln

ii. Indirect heating — cooking

As we have seen the direct heating techniques have a number of limitations. The most fundamental improvement that can be made is to separate the kiln into two parts: the furnace, or combustion chamber, and the oven. Given this simple division there is a whole range of designs possible incorporating more or less independent improvements to the two elements.

• Flat-plate kiln

These simple kilns are designed for use with gypsum sands. A quantity of sand is spread to a depth of about 80 mm on a steel plate heated from below by a fire and occasionally stirred and turned with a wooden rake. As the temperature rises the molecules of water (the water of crystallization) is driven off and the sand appears to boil. After 30-45 minutes the sand has become lighter in colour and the calcination is complete.

In its basic form the kiln can be very simple and cheap, such as in the Cape Verde example described below. Yet, one of the advantages of the technique is how readily it lends itself to progressive improvement as and when resources permit. In its basic form it has a number of problems:

- The only outlet for the smoke is from around the pan or from the top of the doors to the fuel hole. This can make work unpleasant and may lead to contamination of the plaster.
- The kiln has no through draft so the heating is uneven and the combustion of the fuel incomplete.
- If the steel plate is irregular, as it is if flattened-out oil drums are used, it can be difficult to clean off the plaster.
- An oil drum plate may well have quite a short working life.
- If the heated gypsum is not constantly kept moving it can erupt, sending up fine dust that may get carried away with the wind.
- Because the heated surface is open and exposed the heat loss is relatively high, hence the kiln is not as fuel-efficient as more sophisticated designs.

These problems can be more or less solved by increased sophistication in the design, with the addition of a chimney say, or in the case of the steel plate by better quality.

Not withstanding these deficiencies, the simple construction of the basic flat-plate kiln permits an artisanal gypsum plaster manufacturing operation to get under way with very little cost in time and money *if* there is a ready supply of gypsum sand.

• Open pan kiln

The open pan kiln can be seen as a development from the flat-plate kiln, which through design sophistications and greater expense, solves some of its problems. It has two key features:

- A chimney which creates a draft which: increases combustion; distributes the heat; and heats the plate with hot gases rather than directly with flame, which prolongs the life of the plate.
- Rather than using a flat sheet it uses a pan with high sides which keeps heat in and wind out. It does, however, complicate the process of removing the finished plaster.

CASE STUDY 1: Cape Verde Islands — flat-plate kiln

The Cape Verde Islands have an active salt industry, one of the islands being called the island of salt. Gypsum is often found associated with rock salt and in 1977 the gypsum sands on the island of Maio were being referred to as the 'gypsum problem'. An extensive area of the island was unusable for agriculture because of the presence of an estimated million tons of 95 to 98% pure gypsum sand. With the help of Stefan Cramer of the Geological Institute of the Free University of Berlin the local people converted the 'problem' into a resource for an artisanal industry.

The people of the village of Morrinho formed a co-operative to extract, process and market the gypsum. The sand is dug up with spades from the nearby 'salt plain'. The sand is spread out in a low-walled compound to dry out in the sun. Lumps are broken up and stones removed by passing the sand through a fine sieve made from mosquito netting, giving a maximum particle size of around 1mm.

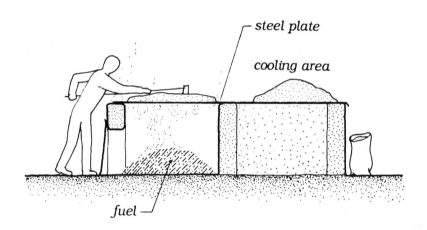

Flat-plate kiln

The calcination is done in the manner described above, over a kiln made from limestone laid in mud mortar, finished with a conventional sand-cement mortar. This is the construction generally used by the villagers for their own houses. The kilns are each approximately 2 m long, 1.5 m wide, and 1 m high. The plates are made from beaten-out oil drums. At the end of each kiln, at the same height as the plate, is a cooling off area to which the freshly calcined powder is raked. Each kiln requires two oil drums and two 50 kg bags of cement. Once cool the plaster is put into 50 kg sacks and is ready for sale, with a profit of 8 %, at a price equivalent to one quarter of the local price for cement. The production costs have been estimated at 73 % salaries, 14 % fuel, and 13 % transport. The initial investment of building the kiln, and of sundries such as the rakes, can be paid off by the profit from 2,600 bags of plaster, which would be about a year's production.

The majority of the work in the co-operative is done by women, since so many of the men migrate for work. A typical team of six women and two men use 1,000 kg of raw gypsum per day and 0.25 kg of firewood per kg of raw gypsum.

CASE STUDY 4: Mauritania — open-pan kiln

Between the years 1982-4 the Association pour le Dévelopement naturel d'une Architecture et d'une Urbanisme Africain (ADAUA) introduced two open-pan kilns for a housing project in Nouakchott, Mauritania. Each pan was made from the steel bucket of an old lorry and was 4 m long by 2.3 m wide. The pan was heated from a fire below and to one side of the pan, the hot gases passing through a simple baffle beneath the pan before being discharged through a chimney made of oil drums. The fuel used was a mixture of wood shavings from local sawmills and used machine oil from a nearby power station.

The gypsum sand is brought to the boil then allowed to cool somewhat before being brought to the boil for a second time. The resulting powder is left to stand in mounds for 15 to 20 days to let the process finish slowly. The finished plaster takes 7 to 10 minutes to reach the initial set, reaching a hard set in 15 to 25 minutes.

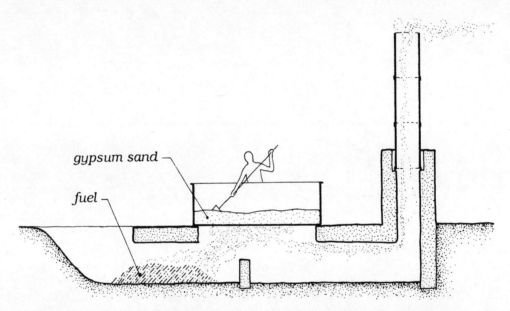

gypsum sand

fuel

Open-pan kiln — Mauritania

In the practice it was found that a team of four men could produce and bag 2.3 tonnes of plaster, in two batches, every day, though this was working a 16-hour day. Put another way each man produced 36 kg per hour. Each kilogram of finished gypsum plaster required 0.1 kg of sawdust and 0.05 litres of oil. The lorry buckets used for the pans had to be replaced every 150 firings, that is one bucket for every 3,450 bags of plaster, each bag being 50 kg.

The quality of the plaster produced was not as high as that in earlier tests in smaller prototypes but was considered sufficient for the proposed uses of plastering walls and as a constituent in hollow floor-blocks.

• Enclosed kilns

Using an enclosed, ventilated, chamber greater fuel efficiency can be achieved and larger quantities processed. As in the previously described kilns, the gypsum requires constant stirring to achieve even calcination and so, except where this can be mechanized, use of these kilns is labour intensive. To avoid 'over-burning' the process has to be carefully controlled, preferably with thermometers and a well-designed adjustable furnace. Because the heating is indirect any kind of heat source may be used, not only solid fuels like coal, charcoal and wood, but also oil and gas, depending on what fuel is most appropriate for a particular location.

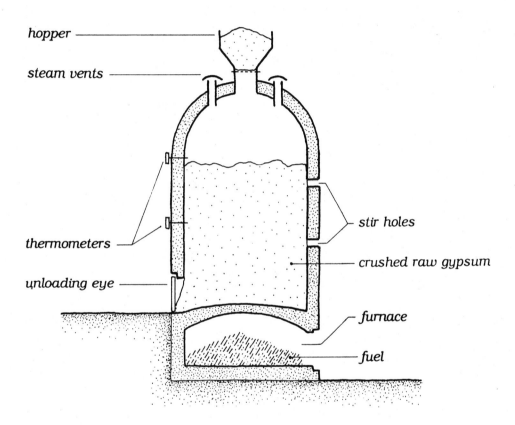

Hopper-fed furnace-heated batch kiln

There are various designs for such kilns, some with simple furnaces beneath the chamber, others with hot gases fed in from holes in the side. By building the kiln in the form of a hopper, with a narrow heating area at the bottom, the gypsum can be processed continuously rather than in batches (as shown overleaf). Such a kiln, producing 25 to 30 tonnes of gypsum plaster per day, was found to consume 70 kg of charcoal for every tonne of gypsum plaster.

The calcined gypsum produced by these more controllable methods is a much better quality than the basic quality, directly fired ash-plaster. It is finer ground, more evenly calcined and is ash-free. Additives can be mixed with this relatively pure gypsum plaster to retard the setting time and to give different types of mix.

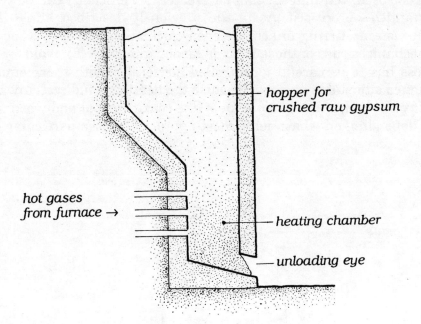

Continuous-production kiln

The strength of this improved-quality gypsum plaster is considerably higher than the basic, and typical crushing strengths are in the order of 60 kg/cm^2; about twice that of the ash plaster produced by direct heating techniques.

• *Kettles*

Modern designs for enclosed kilns using steel chambers are known as kettles. At temperatures around 150 degrees centigrade, the calcination in a typical modern batch kettle with a capacity of 20 tonnes takes $1\frac{1}{2}$ to 2 hours. There are a large number of kettle designs, using different types of fuel and methods of production.

Kettles which produce batches of calcined gypsum are most suited to small-scale operations where production can be geared to changing situations, and where demand for the finished product and supplies of raw material could be variable. Where demand is constant and high, and supplies of raw materials are guaranteed, continuous production is more efficient than batch production. Continuous production conical kettles are the principal means of gypsum plaster production in the industrialized countries. These are highly capital-intensive and require finely ground gypsum and sophisticated control engineering to co-ordinate pump flows, fuel consumption, temperature and pressure.

• *Rotary kiln*

To avoid the necessity of stirring the gypsum within the kiln, the kiln itself can be rotated. Rotary kilns are steel cylinders which are rotated over a source of heat, mixing the gypsum inside with fixed blades. A relatively simple example of this type of system appropriate for medium-scale operations has been developed in the

Platna factory in Noumérate, Algeria, where they achieved plaster with a crushing strength of up to 75 kg/cm². A more sophisticated continuous process, oil-fired, rotary kiln, used in Britain, has an output of 3.5 tonnes per hour.

• *Pressure kilns — autoclaves*

The hemi-hydrate produced by the above methods of heating, in a vessel that is at atmospheric pressure, is known as calcium hemi-hydrate variety β. A stronger variety of hemi-hydrate, known as variety α, can be produced by heating the raw gypsum in a closed container, building up a higher pressure in a saturated atmosphere, usually with a saline solution. The pressure vessels are known as autoclaves. Hemi-hydrate α is considerably stronger than variety β, with a set compressive strength in the order of 500-600 kg/cm²; about 10 times that of the β. It is also faster setting and is able to be hydrated with much less water, allowing a lower water-mix ratio and so developing its higher strengths. For smaller-scale operations autoclaves are not appropriate.

iii. Temperature control

For calcination to happen the temperature must exceed 96°C, but beyond that the process of transformation from gypsum to hemi-hydrate to anhydrite is dependent on a complex interaction of time, temperature and air pressure.

A study in Egypt revealed the following results for samples of gypsum, each heated for given periods at constant temperatures.

Temperature	Time	Results
90°C	1 hour	No change to the gypsum
100°C	1 hour	Partial transformation of gypsum into hemi-hydrate
110°C	1hour	Mainly hemi-hydrate with a little raw gypsum
120°C	1 hour	Hemi-hydrate with significant amounts of anhydrite
100°C	5 hours	Hemi-hydrate with significant amounts of anhydrite
130°C	5 hours	Anhydrite

It can be seen from these figures that quite minor changes can drastically effect the nature of the finished product. The implication of these characteristics is that each new kiln design needs to be tested with different temperatures, different particle sizes, and different stirring regimes, and the resulting plasters tested for their quality, to achieve an optimum working practice to obtain the type of plaster that is desired. (For properties of plasters with different proportions of dihydrate, hemi-hydrate and anhydrite, see section on types of plaster).

5. Economics of production

Those considering making financial investments in the production of gypsum plaster will wish to know whether production will be economically viable. In this section the available information is analysed to assess the relative importance of the different production inputs in small-scale production, and the cost comparison with Portland cement, the principal alternative binding material available everywhere. This will depend on both production cost factors and market factors, and will also be strongly influenced by the local market price of alternative binding materials.

A) Production inputs

Costs of production in local currency in one locality and at one time are not a very useful guide to what might be expected in another place and time. The use of official exchange rates and inflation multipliers can be very misleading. Thus no attempt is made to quote the production costs directly.

Rather, an attempt is made to give an indication of the quantity of the physical inputs needed for some small-scale production processes, relating these to the types of activity involved. Some key inputs to the cost of production are: labour, fuel, transport, and equipment cost or depreciation on investment. Although the information on these inputs is sparse, it does give a general indication of the likely production characteristics.

i. Labour requirements

The amount of labour needed depends on the type of technology used, and particularly on the methods of quarrying used and the extent of mechanization of activities such as materials handling, crushing, and bagging. Some examples, all relating to small-scale production (i.e. less than 10 tonnes per day), are:

- In Maio island, Cape Verde, where building plaster is made from locally dug gypsum sand using a flat-plate kiln process (see case study 3), to produce 750 kg per day, eight people were employed, two men and six women (i.e. approximately ten man-days per tonne).
- In Tessalit, Mali, building plaster is produced in a traditional industry using direct heating kilns at a scale of 100 tonnes per month. Fifteen to twenty people are employed in the factory and another twenty in the quarry, so giving a labour productivity of seven to eight man-days per tonne.
- In the ADAUA (Association pour le Développement naturel d'une Architecture et d'une Urbanisme Africain) factory in Nouakchott, in Mauritania (see case study 4), the cost of labour was thirty per cent of the cost of production; at prevailing wage rates in the region, this is equivalent to nine to eleven man days per tonne.

By comparison the labour productivity of small-scale lime-pozzolana cement production in Africa was found to be between ten and eighteen man-days per tonne.

ii. Fuel

One of the strongest arguments in favour of gypsum plaster is the low temperature of *calcining*, which should be reflected in lower fuel consumption by comparison with lime (around 900°C kiln temperature) and Portland cement (around 1,450°C kiln temperature). However, smaller scale operations tend to have lower fuel efficiencies. Some examples are:

- In the Maio project the cost of fuel was 13 per cent of product cost; the fuel consumption was 0.25 tonnes of local brushwood per tonne of raw gypsum. This suggests an energy consumption of approximately 260 KJ/kg.
- In Tessalit, Mali, each tonne of gypsum plaster requires about 65 litres of light fuel oil; an energy consumption of about 155 KJ/kg.
- In the Nouakchott factory, the cost of fuel was 12 per cent of the total production cost, consisting of a mixture of sawdust and waste oil, both from local sources. Fuel consumption was 105 kg of sawdust and 50 of waste oil for each batch of 1.15 tonnes of gypsum plaster; an estimated energy consumption of 170 KJ/kg.
- Modern production methods require substantially less fuel, 38 to 48 KJ/kg for direct heating methods and 45 to 55 KJ/kg for indirect heating methods.

By contrast, production of Portland cement requires between 240 and 380 KJ per kilogram of cement, depending on the type and scale of technology used.

iii. Transport

The transport cost element of production cost depends primarily on the distance and quality of roads between the factory and the quarry or source of material.

- In Tessalit, where the raw material was 90 km from the factory, transport costs amounted to an estimated 15 to 20 per cent of the cost of production.
- In Nouakchott, the cost of transporting the raw material a distance of 60 km on poor roads to the factory amounted to nearly 40 per cent of the cost of production.
- In Maio, transport by donkey and truck, a total distance not exceeding 10 km, amounted to 13 per cent of the cost of production.

Transport costs from the factory to the point of sale can also be a significant element of the total sales price; in Mali, for example, the selling price of building plaster at the regional town of Gao, 560 km distant, was 60 per cent higher than that at the factory because of transport costs.

iv. Equipment costs and depreciation

The assumed depreciation on equipment depends on the cost and assumed life of kilns, grinders, crushers, vehicles, and any other equipment used. Accurate figures are difficult to obtain because the true equipment cost in production units is not always properly assessed. In Maio, for example, the total equipment cost for the kiln and other equipment was reported to be the same as the cost of production of one tonne of gypsum plaster, and depreciation was ignored in product cost estimates. At Nouakchott, depreciation was estimated at only one per cent of the cost of production, while in another project in Dakar, Senegal, depreciation was calculated at 12 per cent of the production cost.

In *Construire en Plâtre,* Nolhier concluded that in European gypsum plaster factories the capital cost per annual tonne produced is a function of the degree of mechanization, measured by the labour productivity, as shown in the graph below. The capital cost of gypsum plaster production is around 40 to 50 per cent that of cement production. This applies to moderately large-scale rather than very small-scale production.

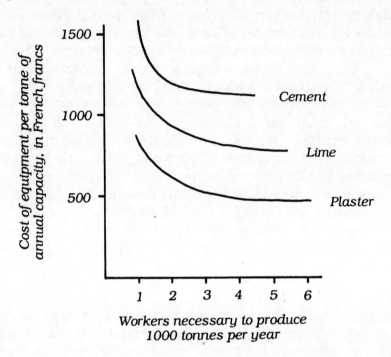

Comparative costs of production of Portland cement, lime and gypsum plaster as a product of the degree of mechanization.

B) Cost comparison with Portland cement

Where potential applications for gypsum plaster overlap with those for Portland cement, it is valuable to obtain an estimate of the relative costs per unit of each material to the user, as a starting point for an economic comparison of the two materials. On the other hand, since the quantities of the two materials used in an application, such as plastering or block production, are not the same, the relative methods and quantities used will need to be taken into account in deciding which material is economically preferable in any situation.

Nolhier has studied the comparative selling prices in six different locations. He concludes that:

• The price of *hemi-hydrate* is close to 60 per cent of the price of cement for developed industries close to each other.

• The relative distance of the production locations from the point of use has a large effect on the relative prices.

• Where gypsum plaster is made in geographically favourable locations, i.e. distant from cement production, it can be sold for 30 per cent of the price of cement.

The last conclusion is confirmed by the experience of the Cape Verde Islands where locally produced gypsum plaster is sold for 25 per cent of the cost of imported cement.

However, the same study shows that the complete costs of two alternative methods of wall construction, one using cement blocks with cement plaster, and the other gypsum plaster blocks with a render of gypsum plaster, are very similar. In one location studied, gypsum plaster based walls cost the same, while in another they cost 20 per cent more than cement based walls of the same performance.

C) Choice of technology
In the building materials industries, studies have shown that in developing countries small-scale production units using local raw materials for local use offer a number of significant advantages:
- The smaller and less stringent raw materials requirements permit small plants to be established in locations unsuitable for large-scale production.
- Smaller-scale production plants can utilize a variety of locally obtainable, often low-grade, fuels.
- Smaller-scale production depends less on purchased energy and more on manual labour than large-scale production.
- Capital costs per unit of output are generally lower for smaller-scale production than for the larger scale.
- Installation, repair and maintenance of small-scale plants can be carried out locally without imported skills, parts or equipment.

The available evidence for small-scale production of gypsum plaster tends to confirm these general observations, and suggests that, because of the lower energy requirements, small-scale production of gypsum plaster may be even more advantageous, in certain circumstances, than small-scale production of Portland cement or lime-pozzolana binders.

However, at the present time, it appears that gypsum plaster produced at a small scale does not offer a significant cost advantage over Portland cement for overall building costs except in very favourable circumstances such as an island economy. The principal economic arguments in favour of establishing gypsum plaster production are:
- It reduces import and capital costs, replacing these with local labour and fuels. These are benefits to the local economy, and offer protection against future unfavourable price movements in the international economy.
- Present technologies of improved small-scale production are in their infancy and thus relatively underdeveloped, and their use of resources is inefficient. As experience develops, it can be expected that production costs will drop substantially, increasing the competitiveness of the small-scale technology.

Use in building

---

1. 'Wet' uses

A) Plastering

Traditionally, the most important use for gypsum plaster has been as a wet applied finish for internal walls and ceilings. Gypsum plaster is mixed with water and trowelled onto the surfaces. In some cases, where labour is expensive, it can be sprayed on.

Gypsum plaster has an intrinsic weakness in external use in that it breaks down in the presence of moisture. However, this does not totally preclude its use externally. Its use as an external render has been traced back to the eighth century BC in Syria and is used extensively throughout the Arab and Mediterranean countries. In the damper climates of Europe its external use has been mainly stimulated by its versatility as a decorative material and its fire-retardant properties.

In Paris, in 1667, because of frequent fires an ordinance was passed obliging house owners to cover the timber frames of houses, inside and out, with nailed laths and gypsum plaster. This legal requirement, combined with the versatility of plaster, stimulated a decorative craft where the façades of timber frame buildings were transformed into elaborate, fashionable, decorated 'stone' façades, with joints carefully carved into the surface of the plaster. The plasters used for this work had to be more resistant to the weather than normal plaster of Paris. The mix developed contained:

      40 kg gypsum plaster
       6 kg lime
      30 kg sand
      25 litres of water

The use of lime increased both the strength and the water resistance of the plaster. It also gave the plaster a very long period until *final* set, allowing the plaster to accommodate the initial settlement of the structure. However, the *initial* set remained relatively rapid.

In Peru, there is a tradition of using an external render, known as *diablo,* for walls and roofs which consists of five parts of gypsum plaster to one part of Portland cement.

Gypsum plaster renders are often mixed with some sort of reinforcement to give it the flexibility to withstand the expansion and contraction stresses that it experiences with changes in moisture content and temperature. Traditional additives of fibrous reinforcements like horse hair or straw have been replaced to some extent by plasticizers and expanded metal meshes in modern construction. Internal renders are sometimes applied onto a reinforcing layer of fabric, e.g. gauze, calico, jute, etc.

B) Plaster mortars

Traditional mortars of gypsum plaster have been used in Western Europe for centuries, to build load-bearing walls of rubble masonry, in North Africa to bind walls of Louz, or sand-roses. Its fast-setting properties make it an ideal mortar for use in the construction of domes and vaults without formwork, where each brick must be supported by other freshly laid bricks. Recent experiments in Lahore, Pakistan have demonstrated the ability of a mortar with a gypsum plaster to sand ratio of 1:3 to achieve setting strengths that comply with national standards for cement-sand mortars. The compressive strength of such a mortar was found to be slightly less than a 1:6 cement-sand mortar, whereas a mortar with a gypsum plaster to sand ratio of 1:2 was significantly stronger. Mortar using plaster of Paris sets very quickly and so has limited workability. The researchers in Lahore used sodium citrate as a retarder, in quantities of 0.02 per cent to 0.05 per cent which gave a setting time of 20 to 40 minutes. The use of plaster mortars in situations where it can become wet is undesirable, and in countries with high rainfall, such as England and France, its use in the foundations of buildings was prohibited in the eighteenth century.

C) Plaster concrete

A very rapid-setting weak concrete can be made by pouring a fluid mix of gypsum plaster over rocks and aggregate, within shutters. Plaster concrete was used in traditional construction by building up layers of sand and gravel between formwork and pouring in gypsum plaster slurry to form lifts of solid walling. The potential for plaster concrete in modern construction is being investigated by the Commune des Regions Sahariennes in Noumérate, Algeria.

The strength was found to be closely linked to the ratio of water to dry plaster weight; the less water the better. A practical optimum was found to be 2 parts water to 5 parts plaster by weight.

In Algerian experiments they have found that it is essential for the plaster to have a retarder. Without one it is impractical to cast a significant-sized piece of concrete in one go. Each batch was 200 litres, which limits the usefulness of plaster concrete as a serious building technique. The other serious problem is the hydraulic pressure of the highly liquid plaster on the formwork. The formwork has to be both strong and well sealed.

D) Decoration

Gypsum plaster is the basis of the traditional plasters used for built-up decorative work. Gypsum plaster can be carved or cast into intricate decorative shapes, such as cornices, ceiling roses etc. They can be pre-fabricated in a workshop or made on site. Large decorative castings are fixed to the structure by setting metal cramps or frames into the wall, and casting the gypsum plaster around them. Decorative mouldings and carvings are a labour-intensive but readily transportable product.

It may be that the production of decorative elements could prove to be a potential export possibility in North Africa with the oil-rich and decoration conscious Arab countries on its door step. Gypsum plaster's fine absorbant surface proved to be an ideal background for the water-colour paintings which came to be known as *frescoes*.

Gypsum plaster carving is an art practised in many areas around the world. In the Middle East craftsman have perfected a technique of making a very hard and fine surface for decorative carving. The plaster is applied in layers. Then, after the initial set of each layer, but before the final set, the surface is beaten with a stone to compact the surface. This technique is extremely time consuming often taking many hours to complete one square metre. But the resulting surface makes possible the intricate and long lasting decorations of so many Islamic buildings.

CASE STUDY 5: Iran — Structural plaster

The technique described here, traditional to Iran, has been described in detail by Xavier Luccioni in the Nolhier's book Construire en Plâtre.

In Iran timber is too scarce to use for roof structures or to make formwork for vaults. A technique has evolved where domes and vaults are built of and around ribs of gypsum plaster reinforced with reeds.

The mason draws out on the ground the shape of half of the arch which he wishes to build. Around this shape he builds two low walls of earth brick. These walls create a mould in which the builder may cast a plaster arch reinforced with a matrix of reed. The semi-arch dries quickly and the walls may be used to cast the other half of the arch, as well as subsequent ones.

Each of the two masonry piers to support the arch are built with a recess to take the foot of the semi-arch. The two halves are placed in their respective recesses, with earth mortar, and the apex of the arch joined with a dab of fresh plaster, which rapidly dries.

To make a barrel vault (a continuous tunnel) a series of independent arches is raised, the gaps being filled with bricks or gypsum plaster blocks. But this form is relatively rare. More common is the low flattened square dome, which is made by raising arches on the four sides, from which a dome is built using earth bricks. Such domes can be linked to form the covered streets of the Iranian markets.

2. Prefabricated elements

A) Plasterboard

The industrialization of building materials in many developed countries over the past half century has resulted in the widespread manufacture of plasterboard. This is a thin layer of gypsum plaster cast between sheets of paper or board. The paper reinforces the plaster, giving it the strength to act as a single sheet. The technology of production is relatively sophisticated, requiring rolling a controlled thickness of plaster mix between two sheets of paper, usually as a continuous production process which is then cut to size. The setting rate of the plaster is critical, and drying time is the limiting factor in many production processes. The end product, a dry finish for walls and ceilings, has many advantages over traditional wet rendering techniques, including rapid coverage of wall area, semi-skilled installation and no waiting time before applying top finishes. The use of plasterboard for internal lining is almost ubiquitous in larger building contracts in industrialized regions. However, in the developing world, where on the whole labour is cheap relative to manufactured goods, the use of plasterboard is less rational.

B) Reinforced gypsum plaster

Gypsum plaster, though relatively strong in compression, is weak in tension. But, as with concrete, the material can be used in conjunction with a material of high tensile strength. Steel reinforcement has, to date, not proved to be very successful, largely because of the poor bond developed between plaster and steel. Yet, there is a long tradition of using fibres, like horse hairs, to reinforce plaster. Experimental programmes in a number of countries are investigating the possibilities of other fibres.

Concrete reinforced with glass fibre requires special alkali-resistant fibres. But plaster has a neutral pH, which means that conventional glass fibres ('E' glass fibres) may be used to make glass-reinforced gypsum plaster (GRG). Such fibres are now manufactured in many of the newly industrializing countries. For instance in Brazil experiments have been carried out on making light-weight wall panels from GRG. In these experiments the plaster and the fibres were augmented with lightweight clay aggregate. The 30 to 60 mm long glass fibres were added to the dry mix in a fibre to plaster ratio of 1:50, by weight, and in Brazil this added about a third to the cost of the unreinforced panel. Experiments in Britain, using higher ratios of fibre to plaster (1:10), indicated that this is up to four times stronger in tension than unreinforced gypsum plaster, while its impact strength can be 20 to 30 times greater. GRG has become an important element of contemporary Islamic architecture since it is an ideal material for highly decorated, repetitive elements such as sun-screens.

Where glass fibres are not a viable proposition vegetable fibres may be a possibility. In Israel experimenters have produced a sisal-reinforced plaster board while prefabrication plants in Australia and Senegal have been used to produce vegetable fibre reinforced gypsum plaster wall units for use on concrete structures in a number of large-scale housing developments.

Apart from using fine fibres gypsum plaster can also be reinforced by using coarser materials. In industrialized countries plaster is often reinforced with steel mesh. In Egypt, Cairo University has experimented with industrial materials, such as wire mesh, glass-wool mat, and polypropylene woven fabric. But they have also made panels reinforced with reeds and burlap. Such panels were found to take loads 50 to 60 per cent greater than unreinforced panels. More work needs to be done to assess the long-term properties of fibre-reinforced gypsum plaster.

CASE STUDY 6: Ecuador — Plaster ceiling panels

The technique described here has been used for at least fifteen years by small commercial workshops in the Ecuadorian Andes to produce decorative ceiling panels.

The ceiling panels drying outside the workshop

The panels are cast in shallow moulds, 1.2 m square, with glass bottoms. On the glass, shapes could be built up, also using glass, to create decorative patterns. Plaster of Paris is mixed with sisal fibre and trowelled into the mould. A frame made from a relatively rigid bamboo-like reed (carizo) is placed on the wet plaster and the plaster is built up around the frame. The finished panels can be nailed to the joists.

The conventional material for ceilings in Ecuador is plywood which is more expensive but more durable than the plaster panels. When made with glass moulds the plaster panels have a very high quality finish. The panels have been found to last well, except in poorly ventilated kitchens and bathrooms in which the surfaces tend to break up (see test for 'soundness').

CASE STUDY 7: Turkey — stabilized block

Professor Ruhi Kafescioglu of the Technical University of Istanbul has carried out a number of experiments with earth blocks stabilized with gypsum plaster, known as 'alker' blocks. Gypsum plaster is widely available in Turkey and is traditionally used as an earth stabilizer. The university's experiments demonstrated that, despite gypsum plaster's inherent weakness in humid conditions, soil blocks made with 10 to 15 % gypsum plaster performed significantly better than normal soil blocks in rain.

Even more impressive were the results obtained indicating dramatic increases of compressive strength. Four soil types were tried from around Istanbul, each with different characteristics.

Soil Type	A	B	C	D
Gravel	8 %	0 %	0 %	25 %
Sand	7 %	10 %	15 %	45 %
Silt	50 %	65 %	54 %	27 %
Clay	35 %	25 %	31 %	3 %

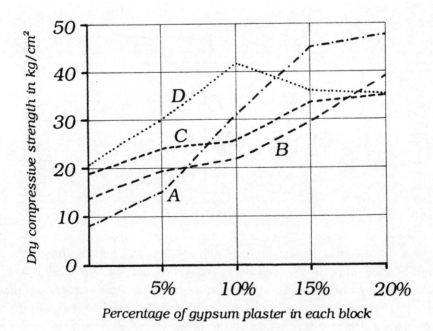

These results confirm that earth blocks stabilized with gypsum plaster are quite suitable for load-bearing applications for up to two-storey buildings. Further experiments indicated that even exposure to heavy rain causes little erosion of blocks stabilized with 10 to 20 % gypsum plaster.

C) Earth blocks stabilized with gypsum plaster

Gypsum plaster can be used as a stabilizer of soil, to improve the binding and durability of soil used in construction. Earth blocks stabilized with gypsum plaster, known as *alker* blocks, are currently being used in the Cape Verde Islands to build load-bearing walls. Where used externally, in damp climates, walls built of alker blocks need to be well protected by means of large overhanging roofs, impervious plinths and water resistant render.

D) Plaster blocks

Gypsum plaster can be cast as building blocks, either as pure gypsum plaster, or more commonly, as gypsum plaster with an aggregate. Pure gypsum plaster blocks are dense, heavy and brittle, and are usually cast as hollow blocks. Aggregates used with gypsum plaster include crushed rock gypsum, limestone or foamed light-weight aggregates. The aggregate makes a lighter block and, if bonded properly, gives additional strength to the block.

CASE STUDY 8: Cape Verde Islands — wall block

The Maio Island artisanal gypsum plaster production project was described earlier. In parallel with the production the project workers introduced new uses for gypsum plaster, primarily a hollow building block. The mix recommended was:

1 part gypsum plaster
1 part clean sand
2 parts gravel
1 part water

(parts by volume)

The mixture was mixed dry first since once wet the plaster sets extremely quickly.

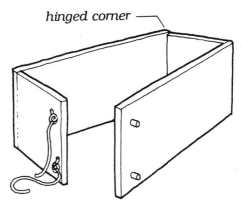

hinged corner

The mould for the blocks

A simple wooden mould was used, made of two 'L' shaped parts hinged together, to make a single brick approximately 400 mm long, 150 mm wide, and 200 mm deep. To reduce weight and cost, two hollows were made using bottles or sticks as formers. After 10 to 15 minutes the brick could be removed from the mould. It was then left to dry in the sun for several days (it has since been suggested that better results would be achieved with a day's damp curing). The mortar recommended was equal parts of plaster and sand with half a part of water.

To promote the use of the blocks the project workers carried out various demonstration projects, principally in the actual houses of the villagers. A house and a co-operative shop had been internally plastered, while the blocks were used to make a new dividing wall in a fisherman's house. Since then blocks have been used to make boundary walls and external walls as well as partitions. It appears the blocks have caught on better than gypsum plaster used for internal plastering. The gypsum plaster block walls were finished inside and out with sand/cement render.

Gypsum plaster blocks are used traditionally in North African countries (examples of many buildings constructed in gypsum plaster blocks can be seen in Ouargla and Noumérate in Algeria) and much experimentation is currently being carried out on their suitability for wider use in other gypsum-rich countries. A programme of experimentation on aggregates and material strengths of gypsum plaster blocks is currently being carried out in Turkey by the Government General Directorate of Materials Research. The use of gypsum plaster blocks for structural purposes is limited by their loss of strength as their moisture content rises. For infill construction, a major use of concrete blocks, gypsum plaster blocks have many advantages over concrete blocks in thermal insulation and acoustic density.

Where more capital-intensive production is viable, spanning floor blocks can be made. In Senegal and Algeria experimental houses have used hollow gypsum plaster blocks, typically 500 x 200 x 160 mm, to span between reinforced concrete beams.

Vaulted constructions can be made, without any formwork, using a light-weight hollow plaster 'briquette' laid in a quick setting plaster mortar. It is reported that a team of three masons using this technique can cover more than 10 m^2 per day.

Glossary

---

accelerator A substance added to *gypsum plaster* to accelerate the process of setting. This is particularly useful in the production of plasterboard.

anhydrite $CaSO_4$, calcium sulphate, that is, *gypsum* with all the molecules of water driven out.

calcining The process of chemical change through heating, in particular the change from *dihydrate* to *hemi-hydrate* with water as a by-product. The same term is used for the production of lime (CaO) from calcium carbonate ($CaCO_3$) with carbon dioxide (CO_2) as a by-product.

cement see *Portland cement*.

clay Fine grained earth (particles less than 0.002 mm), usually containing silica, alumina and water.

crystal water The molecules of water (H_2O) which link with calcium sulphate ($CaSO_4$) to form *dihydrate* or *hemi-hydrate*.

density The *mass* of an object divided by its volume. This is usually expressed in kg/m^3. If the density is calculated in grams/cm^3 the result can be converted to kg/m^3 by multiplying by one thousand. Water is usually taken to have a density of 1000 kg/m^3.

dihydrate $CaSO_4.2H_2O$, the principal component of raw *gypsum*.

gypsum A naturally occurring mineral, principally consisting of $CaSO_4.2H_2O$, calcium sulphate *dihydrate*.

gypsum plaster A building material, consisting predominantly of *hemi-hydrate*, usually with some *anhydrite*, some *dihydrate*, and other impurities or chemical *retarders* or *accelerators*.

hemi-hydrate $CaSO_4.\frac{1}{2}H_2O$, produced by *calcining* raw *gypsum,* when in a virtually pure state it is known as *plaster of Paris*.

knocking back This is the process whereby a plasterer mixes in more water to his batch of drying plaster to maintain its workability. This is only possible with plasters containing a high proportion of *anhydrite* or other *retarder*.

lime Limestone, if *calcined* (at 900 to 1,100°C), turns into calcium oxide, also known as quicklime. If this is then wetted (slaked) it breaks down into a fine powder of calcium hydroxide, or hydrated lime also known as slaked lime. In this document the word lime is always used to refer to hydrated lime.

loam   Rich soil composed of sand, clay, silt and humus.

mass   For general purposes, the mass of an object can simply be taken as its weight in kilograms or grams.

plaster   Strictly speaking, plaster is synonymous with *gypsum plaster*, however, in common usage it has come to be used for other thick surface finishes such as 'lime plaster'.

plaster of Paris   *Gypsum plaster* which is virtually 100 per cent *hemi-hydrate*.

Portland cement   Produced by: burning a mixture of limestone and clay, and sometimes bauxite, at a temperature of 1,450°C; adding a small amount of *gypsum*; and grinding to a fine powder.

pozzolana   Materials containing silica and alumina which will react with lime to form a cement-like product. Typical pozzolanas include some kinds of volcanic ash, fuel ash from power stations, blast furnace slag, burnt rice husks, and ground up burnt-clay bricks.

render   A render is any kind of surface finish applied in liquid or semi-liquid form. However, in building it generally applies to a mortar coating.

retarder   A substance added to *gypsum plaster* to slow down the process of setting to make it easier to use.

specific gravity   The ratio of the density of a substance to that of water. For general purposes, it is the *density* of the substance expressed in grams per millilitre (cubic centimetre).

stucco   Stucco is synonymous with *gypsum plaster,* but generally it has come to be associated with fine decorative work formed by building up three-dimensional surfaces from gypsum plaster.

A note on units

Stress 1 kg/cm^2 is approximately equal to 0.1 Newtons per square millimetre (N/mm^2) or 14.5 lb/in^2.

Energy   1 kilojoule (KJ) is equal to 0.239 Kcal or 0.278×10^{-3} KW.h

Selected bibliography

Principal sources

Bardin, F, 1982, *Le Plâtre: Sa Production et Son Utilisation dans l'Habitat,* Groupe de Recherche et d'Echanges Technologiques (GRET), Dossier Technologies et Développement, Ministère de la Coopération et du Développement, Paris.

Nolhier, M., 1986, *Construire en Plâtre,* L'Harmattan, Villes et Entreprises, Paris.

Smith, R.G., 1974, 'Gypsum', Chapter 9 in *Lime and Alternative Cements,* (ed. R.J.S. Spence), Intermediate Technology Publications Ltd., London.

Other publications

Agopyan, V., 1986, *GRG Prepared by Premixing for Wall Panels in Developing Countries,* Instituto de Pesquisas Tecnológicas do Estado de São Paulo, São Paulo.

Blakey, F.A., 1961, 'Cast Gypsum as a Structural Material', *Archit. Sci. Rev.* **4.1,** 6-16. Australia

British Gypsum, 1986, *The White Book: Technical Manual of Building Products,* Nottingham.

British Standards Institution, 1973, *Specification for Gypsum Building Plasters, BS 1191 : Parts 1 & 2 : 1973,* British Standards Institute, London.

Cramer, S., 1982, *Gypsum Production on Maio Island - A New Building Material for Cape Verde?,* Projecto de Gêsso; Institut für Geologie, Berlin.

CSTB, 1985, *Construire en Plâtre dans les Pays en Développement,* Extrait du Magazine CSTB No. 36, Centre Scientifique et Technique du Batiment, Paris.

Everett, A., 1986, 'Fibres and fibre-reinforced products', chapter 10 in *Materials,* Mitchell's Publishing Company, London.

Everett, A., 1979, 'Plastering', chapter 13 in *Finishes,* Batsford, London.

Indian Standards Institution, 1964, *Method of test for Gypsum Plaster, Concrete and Products, IS:2542 (Part I),* Indian Standards Institution, New Delhi.

Kafescioglu, R., 1984, 'Conclusions of the Research for Gypsum Stabilized Adobe (Alker) and an Application', *International Colloquium on Earth Construction Technologies Appropriate to Developing Countries,* Brussels.

King, G.A., 1979, 'Gypsum Products and their Application in the Australian Building Industry', *Symposium on New Building Materials and Components,* Baghdad.

Mahmoud, A et al, 1982, 'Reinforced Gypsum for Egyptian Housing', *Journal of the American Society of Civil Engineers,* **ST6,** pp 1336-1356.

Mohammad, A., and Iqbal, M.Z., 1982, 'Gypsum in Unit Masonry Construction and Plaster Works', *Proceedings of the MTEC '86 conference on materials, construction techniques and construction economy,* Paris.

OCRS, 1982, *Le Plâtre dans la Construction au Sahara,* Organisation Commune des Regions Sahariennes (OCRS), Algiers.

Smith, R.G., 1982, 'Small-scale production of gypsum plaster for building in the Cape Verde Islands', *Appropriate Technology,* 8(4), pp 4-6, Intermediate Technology Publications, London.

Spence, R.J.S., and Cook, D.J., 1983, 'Gypsum, Lime and Pozzolanas', Chapter 6 in *Building Materials in Developing Countries,* John Wiley & Sons, London.

Suain, H., 1982, *Tessalit: Le Plâtre au Mali,* Direction Nationale de l'Urbanisme et de la Construction, Ministère des Transports et des Travaux Publics, Republique du Mali (available from UNCHS - Habitat, Nairobi.)

Contact addresses

Algeria Centre National d'Etudes et de Recherches Integrées du Bâtiment (CNERIB), Cité Nouvelle, El Mokrahi/Wilaya de Tipaza, Souidania.
Source of information on the use of gypsum plaster in north Africa.

Brazil Instituto de Pesquisas Tecnológicas do Estado de São Paulo, São Paulo, SP, CEP 05508, Caixa Postal 7141.
Researchers into fibre-reinforced gypsum plaster.

Egypt Cairo University Faculty of Engineering, Department of Architectural Engineering, Gizah.
Researchers into fibre-reinforced gypsum plaster.

France Centre Scientifique et Technique du Bâtiment (CSTB), 4 Avenue du Recteur Poincaré, 75782, Paris
In 1985 CSTB organized a seminar on gypsum plaster manufacture and use in developing countries.

France Groupe de Recherche et d'Echanges Technologiques (GRET), 21 rue La Fayette, 75010, Paris.
GRET are the publishers of Bardin's book on gypsum plaster production, which is the most comprehensive work available.

France Syndicat National des Industries du Plâtre, 3 Rue Alfred Roll, 75017 Paris.
A source of information on gypsum processing machinery.

India Indian Standards Institution, Manak Bhavan, 9 Bahadur Shah Zafar Marg, New Delhi, 110001.
Developers of low-cost testing techniques for building materials.

Kenya United Nations Centre for Human Settlements (Habitat), PO Box 30030, Nairobi.
A source of literature on building materials and practices.

Mauritania Societé de Construction et de Gestion Immobilière de Mauritanie (SOCOGIM), PO Box 28, Nouakchott.
A source of information on gypsum exploitation and other building materials and practices in Mauritania.

Pakistan Building Research Station, University of the Punjab, New Campus, Lahore 20.
Researchers into the use of gypsum plaster mortars.

Turkey Building Materials Unit, Faculty of Civil Engineering, Istanbul Technical University, Istanbul.
Researchers on the production and use of gypsum plaster stabilized earth blocks (alker blocks — see case study 7)

United Kingdom British Gypsum Ltd., Research and Development Projects, East Leake, Loughborough, Leicestershire LE12 6QJ.
British Gypsum Ltd. are major producers of building plaster and plaster-board, their research and development division are experts on the chemistry of plaster and of gypsum bearing rocks.

United Kingdom Building Research Establishment, Garston, Watford WD2 7JR.
The BRE has carried out a number of studies on gypsum both in Britain and in other countries, including an evaluation of the Cape Verde project (see case study 1).

United Kingdom Cambridge Architectural Research Ltd., 6 Chaucer Road, Cambridge, CB2 2EB
Researchers and consultants on processes and technologies for housing projects in developing countries.

United Kingdom Engineering Laboratory Equipment, Eastman Way, Hemel Hempstead, Hertfordshire, HP2 7HB.
Manufacturers of laboratory equipment.

United Kingdom Intermediate Technology Publications, 103/105 Southampton Row, London WC1B 4HH
IT publications produce literature on various other cementitious materials such as lime and pozzolanas.

United Kingdom Intermediate Technology Development Group, Myson House, Railway Terrace, Rugby, CV21 3HT
Advisors on technology development and applications.

United Kingdom Intermediate Technology Workshops, J.P.M.Parry & Associates Ltd., Overend Road, Cradley Heath, Warley, West Midlands, B64 7DD
Producers of pendulum crushers and other low-cost machinery for the production of building materials and components (see case study 2).

United Kingdom Rockshield Lattis, Vaenor Park, Llandloes, Powys, SY18 6DN
Manufacturers of glass-fibre reinforced gypsum plaster decorative panels and screens.

United Kingdom Sturtevant Engineering Company Ltd., Hamlyn House, Highgate Hill, London, N19 5PP.
Manufacturers of crushing and grinding machinery.